HOW TO USE THIS BOOK

This book is set up to show you, in words and picture[...] [s]cenic miles. The route we take follows Highway One from Monte[...] [incl]udes the superb "circle of enchantment" around the Monte[...] from Monterey to Pacific Grove, along the 17-Mile Drive and [...] to Carmel.

For maximum usefulness, we've designed this book so you can use it whether headed north or south. If you are starting in Monterey, simply begin on page 2 and use the numbers within the BLUE arrow symbol. Mileage marker "zero" in the north is the intersection of Del Monte Avenue and Highway One (the entrance to Monterey).

If you are setting out from Morro Bay, start at the back of the book and use the numbers on the ORANGE arrow symbol. Mileage marker "zero" in the south begins at the Morro Bay Boulevard exit in Morro Bay.

124 miles to San Francisco

139
0

TABLE OF CONTENTS

Historic photos courtesy of: the Pat Hathaway Collection, Glen Bickford, the Monterey Public Library, the Monterey County Library.
Special thanks: master sand-castle builders Wes and Leah Ward, Carl Hansen, Emil White, Capt. Gary Robertson, Bruce Leonard and the California Department of Transportation, Joe Johnson and the Monterey Public Library, Reggie Bradford, Bob Cross and Deborah Johansen, Cliff at the Santa Barbara Museum of Natural History, Tom Scanlon and the Seaside Chamber of Commerce, the Monterey Aquarium, the U.S. Coast Guard, Monterey City Hall, and the California Department of Parks and Recreation, Hearst Castle and Monterey County divisions.

214 miles to Los Angeles   *12 miles to San Luis Obispo*

"At dawn its majesty is
almost painful to behold.
That same prehistoric look.
The look of always.
Nature smiling at herself
in the mirror of eternity."
— Henry Miller,
*Big Sur and the Oranges
of Hieronymus Bosch*

**Pfeiffer Beach, one of Big Sur's
wild and enchanted spots.**

CALIFORNIA
SCENIC HWY 1
MONTEREY to MORRO BAY

PHOTOGRAPHER
HARA

WRITER AND SERIES EDITOR
Vicki León

BOOK DESIGN
Matthew Whittlesey

MONTEREY

139 / 0 Monterey is justifiably called "the place where California began", a luminous little city that sits like a pearl on the lip of indigo Monterey Bay. Since its establishment in 1770, the city has looked to the sea and lived from it. Its once-famous sardine fishing, immortalized by John Steinbeck, has now given way to squid fishing, Monterey's most important marine harvest. (Don't pass up the *calamari* fixed Italian style if you want to learn how good squid can be.)

Not far from the salty charm of Fisherman's Wharf, you can visit what's left of Monterey's own "Plymouth Rock", an ancient oak tree that stood near the water when the first Spanish explorer landed in 1602. Beneath its branches, Sebastián Vizcaino held the first Mass in California. In 1770, the tree again served as a landmark and altar for mission-founder Junipero Serra and explorer Gaspar de Portolá.

Capital of California and main port of call during the Spanish and Mexican eras, Monterey boasts the finest collection of 18th and 19th-century buildings in the state. Take time to stroll along its rewarding "Path of History", to smell the fragrance of jasmine and good Mexican cooking, to delight in its textures of adobe and weathered wood. Monterey will win you over, just as it did Robert Louis Stevenson and countless others.

CANNERY ROW

136 3 Even in its pungent heyday of the 1930s, Cannery Row was never a place of conventional beauty. Instead it was as John Steinbeck described: "a stink, a grating noise, a quality of light," a raffish quarter populated by characters like Doc and Wide Ida and Lee Chong.

The canning era began about 1900 and peaked 40 years later, when the Row's 16 canning and 14 reduction plants processed a quarter of a million tons of sardines annually. Over 70 purse seiners (such as the *Geraldine-Ann,* pictured at right, loaded to the gunwales with 160 tons of silvery catch) worked the bay. But by the 1950s, the sardines had disappeared, probably due to over-fishing. One by one, the canneries closed, and the Row became a gaunt and ghostly relic.

Its reason for existence gone, the Row would no doubt have vanished if it had not been for the popularity of Steinbeck's prize-winning books, *Cannery Row* and *Sweet Thursday.* Today Cannery Row hums with new life: cafés, specialty shops and the aquarium, which displays the denizens of Monterey Bay in the recycled setting of the old Hovden Cannery.

GERALDINE-ANN   GERALDINE-ANN

THE AQUARIUM

136
3

The sardines in the Bay may have disappeared, but you can still see schools of them, alive and well and shimmering through the Kelp Forest exhibit at the Monterey Bay Aquarium.

Using the 1916 Hovden Cannery building as a nucleus, the $40 million Aquarium anchors Cannery Row, adding an attractive and appropriate dimension to a historic district. Within its gray walls, the Aquarium harbors more than 5,000 creatures. Over 300 species are represented, nearly all of them native to Monterey Bay.

Visitors get to view — and even touch — the creatures in the context of their natural habitats. You can pet a velvety bat ray, examine the underside of a sea star, taste a kelp frond. The biggest draw may be the Kelp Forest exhibit, a 3-story, 335,000-gallon tank with its own surge machine. Like its redwood counterpart, the kelp forest has a cathedral-like tranquility. Schools of fish weave among its golden strands, a beautiful refuge for a multitude of marine citizens.

And all of this — 83 exhibits, tidal basin, videos, life-size models — perches on the lip of Monterey Bay, one of the richest marine regions in the world.

PACIFIC GROVE

135 / 4 Founded in 1875 as a religious and cultural retreat, Pacific Grove possesses a beautiful legacy of old churches and frothy Victorian homes from that era. Another of the city's proud possessions is its shoreline: three miles of tidepool-rich beaches, rock formations and flower-carpeted cliffs. Around Lover's Point, Berwick Park and Shoreline Park are the most spectacular displays of pink *Mesembryanthemum chilense* or sea-fig. This magnificent wash of color began as an experimental planting in 1943 and now blooms lavishly, April to July.

Pacific Grove is mysteriously congenial to more than sea-fig. Between October and March, its eucalyptus groves become the wintering ground for millions of Monarch butterflies, who drift here at a cruising speed of 10 mph from points as distant as 1,000 miles north. (In bygone days, particularly shrewd butterflies used to "hitch-hike" south on the rigging of slow-moving sailing ships off Alaska!) This annual event provokes genuine wonder when you realize that none of these golden visitors has ever been here before — a Monarch's life span being 9-10 months. If you're here in season, look but please don't touch. To protect its nectar-sipping friends, Pacific Grove imposes a ferocious $500 fine for butterfly molestation.

At the tip of the peninsula is Point Pinos, long a landmark for Spanish galleons. Since 1855, its lighthouse has endeavored to keep ships off the savage rocks — not always with success, as this picture of an 1896 shipwreck will attest.

ASILOMAR BEACH

132 / 7 On the north and west sides of the Monterey peninsula, the waves tear at the rocks with unbridled enthusiasm. As you round the point and head south, you encounter stretches of sand among the rock formations. Here and there, the sea relents a little, and allows you to peer into its looking-glasses: the tidepools.

Twice a day at low tide, you can readily observe the hustle and bustle of tidepool life, as population-dense as any city. Tidepool dwellers generally make their living in one of four ways: as predators (starfish, sea urchins, sea anemones), filter feeders (mussels, gooseneck barnacles), algae eaters (goby fish, periwinkles) or scavengers (hermit crabs).

Tidepool residents are an eccentric, interdependent bunch. The common green anemone gets its color from tiny algae who live inside its tissues. The blobby sea slug hunts the anemone, unconcernedly absorbing its stinging cells to use as part of its own defense. Shipworms and piddocks are bivalves with even weirder dietary tastes. The former lives on wood; the latter, on rocks.

Because ocean waters from north and south merge here, Asilomar's tidepools probably contain the richest assortment of life-forms along the California coast. If you cared to do so, you could identify 210 different species of algae in them. One of the loveliest is the sea palm, pictured above.

The green anemone gets its color from tiny plants which live inside its tissues.

"...When the tide goes out the little water world becomes quiet and lovely... Anemones expand like soft and brilliant flowers, inviting any tired and perplexed animal to lie for a moment in their arms...The smells of life and richness, of death and digestion, of decay and birth, burden the air."

from John Steinbeck's description of The Great Tidepool at Asilomar

17-MILE DRIVE

131 / 8 A study in contrasts, this portion of the peninsula is famous for its deep pine-filled forest, its five world-class golf courses, its palatial homes and its Bird and Seal Rocks, quivering with abundant animal life.

In the 1800s, the grandnephew and namesake of inventor Samuel F.B. Morse was instrumental in the preservation of the area. On the choicest land, he built the Del Monte Lodge, laid out golf courses and parkland without desecrating forest and established the 17-Mile Drive as a green belt.

For many years, this scenic circuit was an all-day carriage ride. Passengers had a lunch stop at a Chinese fishing village to eat and purchase souvenirs, such as those sold in this photograph of the period. (Strong-minded guests of the Lodge — like Teddy Roosevelt — rode the nearly 35-mile loop on horseback.)

Along a two-mile stretch between Cypress and Pescadero Points, you will find the photogenic and much-photographed Monterey cypresses. Of them, Carmel poet Robinson Jeffers liked to say: "the sailor wind weaves them into deep sea knots." Frail in appearance, the cypresses may be as much as 500 years old. Estimates are rough because this species does not always add a ring annually.

CARMEL

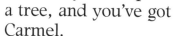 Few settlements in the US have deliberately set out to remain villages. Fewer still have achieved that goal in Carmel's extraordinary fashion. Try to picture a hamlet of highly original houses and small shops, tucked among huge solemn cypresses, the whole thing overlooking the sands of Carmel Bay. Summon up, if you can, a town of 5,000 that permits no neon signs, parking meters, high rises, street lights or plastic plants. Imagine a village that considers it a felony to chop down a tree, and you've got Carmel.

Originally an inexpensive haven for writers and artists, Carmel — whose lots sold for $20 apiece in 1888 — has become fashionable and affluent. Over 100 art and photography galleries now line its wooded streets. The village has also become a mecca for shoppers and restaurant-goers seeking the unusual.

But Carmel's two biggest attractions remain free: its beach and its mission. Each year, a Sand-Sculpture contest — one of the best in California — is held on its sugar-white sands.

Second in the California mission chain, Mission San Carlos Borromeo de Carmelo is second to none in beauty. Now a basilica, Carmel Mission was Father Junipero Serra's favorite. (At the mission, you can visit his burial place, personal library and cell-like living quarters.) Once you've seen its bell towers of dusky gold, its romantic fountains and courtyards, its poignant cemetery, Carmel Mission may become your favorite, too.

PT. LOBOS MARINE RESERVE

116 / 23 Robert Louis Stevenson, who used Point Lobos as a setting for *Treasure Island,* called this headland "the most beautiful meeting of land and sea on earth." Many visitors would agree. Forming the southern arm of Carmel Bay, the Reserve contains 1,276 acres of bold rock, restless water, intimate coves, delicate little beaches, and numerous islets jammed with noisy birdlife and two varieties of sea lions.

It was the non-stop barking of the sea lions that prompted Spanish explorers to name it "Punta de los Lobos Marinos" or "Sea Wolves' Point." (When you think about it, neither "sea lion" nor "sea wolf" suits these creatures very well.)

Point Lobos represents nature at its most sunny and prodigal, a landscape crowded with little kingdoms of sea otters and squirrels, pelicans and bobcats. Over 300 species of plants thrive together, from the world's most superb natural stand of Monterey cypress to ethereal fairy-lantern flowers. Some 178 species of vertebrates and 88 species of marine invertebrates call Point Lobos home.

Birds of various feathers flock together here. Among them: loons, cormorants, grebes, herons and four varieties of gulls. Small wonder that "Jonathan Livingston Seagull" was shot on location at Point Lobos, using winged residents as "extras."

Given the reserve's size and variety of things to see and do, it makes sense to plan a lengthy stop. Don't miss China Cove — where swimming is allowed — and Dillon Beach, where it is not. They are two of California's most perfect beaches. A further plus: their sheltered locations make them pleasant even on windy and overcast days.

At least 14 species of gulls reside in California. As the pictures show, gulls pass through distinct stages of plumage on their way to adulthood. At two years, they lose their protective markings and become sleek white and grey adults.

PT. LOBOS

116 / 23 Point Lobos hasn't always been a serene and unmarked wilderness reserve. Its protected status dates from 1933, when its last owners made it a trust of the state.

Prior to that, Point Lobos served as the shipping point for a coal mine, a rum-running center, a proposed townsite, a dairy ranch, and a favorite locale for film-makers.

But the most interesting (if horrifying) use occurred during the mid-1880s, when Point Lobos was a whaling station. (Near Whaler's Cove, you can still glimpse the whitewashed remains of an old whaler's cabin.)

Whalers began by hunting the California gray, a gentle giant of 50 tons in weight, 35-48 feet in length, with tail flukes ten feet wide. During its annual 13,000-mile round trip from the Arctic seas to Baja California, the gray chugs south from November through February, north in March and April. The tranquil lagoons of Mexico serve as its birthing and breeding grounds.

Their breeding habits, their sedate speed of 4 knots per hour, and their habit of hugging the shoreline made the grays easy prey for the hunters. By 1874, the California gray was nearly extinct, and the whalers turned their attention to the 48- to 52-foot humpback whale. Pictured is a mature humpback being flensed or stripped of its blubber by a Portuguese crew. Both the gray and the humpback were killed for

When the gray whale became scarce, California whalers hunted the humpback. Pictured are the enormous tail flukes of a diving humpback whale.

oil alone, which was clumsily rendered by boiling the blubber in huge pots.

In 1875, whaler Charles Scammon vividly described the sights, sounds and smells of Point Lobos:

"Under a bluff close to the water's edge is the station...the try-works, sending forth volumes of thick black smoke...the shapeless and half-putrid mass of a mutilated whale...the men shouting and heaving on the capstans...the screaming of the gulls mingled with the noise of the surf about the shores..."

Like the sea otter, the story of the gray whale has a happy ending. Both were hunted to seeming extinction. But thanks to the resilience of Mother Nature, a tiny core of breeding animals survived. Today both the sea otter and the California gray whale thrive as protected species.

BIXBY CREEK BRIDGE

105 / 34 The building of Coastal Highway One is full of eye-popping statistics, not the least of which is Bixby Creek Bridge, also called "Rainbow" for its beautiful arch. Measuring 718 feet in length and 260 feet high, Bixby required 600,000 pounds of reinforcing steel and 6,600 cubic yards (825 truckloads!) of concrete. To shape the arch, engineers built an elaborate wooden falsework (pictured here in May 1932) which itself consumed 300,000 board feet of Douglas fir.

LEWIS JOSSELYN;
from PAT HATHAWAY COLLECTION

The first car drove across Bixby Bridge on November 27, 1932, but it was not until 1937 that the entire 139-mile stretch of highway was finished.

Like the road itself, the official opening of Highway One on June 27, 1938, was, well, unconventional. The ceremonies began with a toast to President Roosevelt, a pigeon release, a barbecue, and the appearance of a Pony Express rider. "Local talent" at the ceremony included trained seals, who presented California Governor Frank Merriam with a "manifesto."

Originally budgeted at $1.5 million, the winding road with 33 bridges ended up costing $71,000 per mile — about $10 million. Construction took from 1919 to 1937, partly because funds were a slow-trickling mix of state bonds, gas tax revenues and Federal dollars. Progress was also slow because of engineering problems and the unpredictable weather.

District Engineer Lester Gibson oversaw the project, devoting 7,000 days of his life to it. But the real "father" of this highway was Dr. John Roberts. In 1887, he came to Monterey, a physician's diploma in one pocket and a silver dollar in the other. Soon he was making house calls on horseback along Big Sur. At that time, it had nothing but a bad wagon track to the south end of Big Sur Valley. On his own, Roberts mapped and photographed the territory between Carmel and San Simeon. In 1915, he and Senator Rigdon of San Luis Obispo took his work before the state legislature and persuaded them to appropriate funds. Twenty-two years later, Roberts was among the dignitaries to proudly watch the inauguration of Highway One.

LITTLE SUR RIVER and PICO BLANCO

101 38 For centuries, this was the land of the Sargenta-Ruc, the Eagle-House nation of Costanoan Indians. From their villages at Bixby and Rocky Creeks, they controlled the coast from Palo Colorado Canyon to the mouth of the Big Sur River. Their territory was dominated by 3,709-foot Pico Blanco, the largest body of pure limestone in California. On its white slopes, the Indians believed, the race of man began, aided by an eagle, a hummingbird, and a coyote.

Once the Spanish began land exploration in the 1700s, the entire wild region from Carmel south began to be called "El Pais Grande del Sur" — the Great Land of the South. Its two rivers got the unimaginative names of "Rio Grande" (Big River) and "Rio Chiquito" (Little River) of the South. A mix of American and Spanish usage eventually produced the hybrid names of Big and Little Sur.

This expanse of meadow and river lagoon has seen much history. In 1834, Little Sur River became the northern boundary of Rancho El Sur, a Mexican land grant of 8,949 acres. Once the rancho era came to an end, the area was settled (and sometimes fought over) by a succession of squatters and pioneering families. Despite the beauty of Little Sur beach, you will have to be content with a view from the roadside. The entire area is private property.

PT. SUR LIGHTHOUSE

99 / 40 At Point Sur, a long sandy arm of beach juts southwest into the water, massing itself into a great, 400-foot-high fist of volcanic rock. This pugnacious point of land has been responsible for many shipwrecks, including the spectacular sinking of the S.S. *Los Angeles* in 1894. Not all of the shipwrecks at Point Sur occurred solely in the water. In 1935, the 785-foot dirigible *Macon* crashed here. Quick work by the lighthouse keeper saved all but two of the 83-man Navy crew.

In 1889, local ranchers erected the first kerosene-oil-powered light, painfully building 395 wooden steps up the rock. Early lighthouse keepers got their supplies from Castro Ranch, whose wagons would labor up the 11.2% grade carrying deer meat, beef, tortillas, beans and enchiladas.

Today's 50-foot-high lighthouse looms whitely above the sea, piercing the dark with a million-candlepower beam every 15 seconds. The sound of its compressed-air fog diaphone carries for 10 miles. These facts haven't always impressed everyone. After construction, an elderly Indian named Choppy Casuse was heard to say: "Good light, but she no work. Foghorn all time go booboo, but fog she creep in just the same."

The most breathtaking view of Point Sur and its lonely beach is from the high, cypress-framed bluff one mile north of the Naval Facility road.

Another vantage point is from Hurricane Point, three miles north. At low tide, you once could see a graveyard of 18th and 19th-century shipwrecks on Point Sur's beach. Today, however, 800 feet below Hurricane Point, you can see a graveyard of another sort: the shattered remains of numerous cars which have gone over the edge.

"It was always a wild, rocky coast, desolate and forbidding to the man of the pavements..."

Henry Miller

Now automated, the lighthouse and surrounding land are military property — no visitors. This wind-lashed point also has underwater monitors to detect the sound of ships' propellers.

ALONG THE BIG SUR RIVER VALLEY

94 45 For many decades, Big Sur families had just one source for supplies — a steamer that stopped twice a year. As late as 1920, it took 11 hours to travel from Big Sur's little post office to Monterey, using two good horses and a light wagon. News of the outbreak of World War II reached Big Sur in Paul Revere fashion, on horseback. Electricity took a little longer (1945).

Like its deeply scissored coast, the Big Sur River valley is as isolated as it is beautiful, a place rich in visual treasure yet poor in opportunities to make a living.

As a result, the people who have settled here have really wanted to do so: a self-reliant, adventurous breed who prefer the challenge and solitary grandeur of Big Sur. The basically non-existent "village" of Big Sur is the best example in California of a completely decentralized settlement. You'll find its stores, restaurants and community buildings scattered like breadcrumbs along the Big Sur River. Most of them fall between Andrew Molera State Park to the north and Deetjen's Big Sur Inn to the south.

Besides strenuously maintaining their non-village status, Big Sur residents relish their privacy. And they always have, as this 1905 picture (below) shows. The redoubtable woman with the flower in her hair and the welcoming rifle in her hand is Mary Sweatman, the cabin's owner.

Big Sur residents also maintain a warm controversy over what constitutes "Big Sur." You'll get the fewest arguments if you call the portion south from Carmel to Big Sur Valley "the north coast," and the remaining 60 miles or so to San Simeon, "the south coast."

The Big Sur River drains a 46-square-mile area and has been flowing in this region for over one million years. Like the area's human residents, the river is an independent thinker, periodically changing its course and overflowing its banks. At Molera State park, it flows through 2,154 acres of naturally maintained woodland, estuary and primitive camping. South of Molera, the redwoods begin, the highway passing alternately from shade into sunlit meadows.

The Big Sur coast: graced by the slender silver chain of Highway One, which winds through the Big Sur River Valley before emerging at Nepenthe to hug the water once again.

PFEIFFER-BIG SUR STATE PARK

92 / 47 Named for area pioneer John Pfeiffer, this park shelters glorious stands of coastal redwoods and a substantial stretch of the Big Sur River within its 821 acres. At Pfeiffer-Big Sur, you need a new vocabulary just to describe the greens: emerald green of the maidenhair fern, grey-green eucalyptus, young-frog-green of the sorrel, mallard green of the feathery redwood.

Coastal redwoods (*Sequoia sempervirens*) are the world's tallest living things. The real giants are found near Eureka in northern California, but these specimens are superlative in their own right. First noted and named by the Portolá expedition of 1769, the coastal redwoods have been cut down in huge numbers because of the usefulness of their timber.

Although you can get a courtesy permit for a 30-minute drive-through, take the time to walk to Pfeiffer Falls or the Gorge. The ranger-guided walks in summer are especially worthwhile.

Further east, the park links up with Los Padres National Forest and the vast Ventana Wilderness, so named because it is a "ventana" or window into the backcountry of the Santa Lucia Mountains. In it, golden eagles and redtailed hawks soar over rare Santa Lucia bristlecone firs, phantom white orchids, wild boar and the occasional mountain lion.

One mile south of Pfeiffer-Big Sur's entrance is Sycamore Canyon Road, the access to Pfeiffer Beach, two miles west. (Look for a tiny sign, mailboxes, and a narrow, downhill lane.)

This side trip to the beach made famous in the "Sandpipers" film is well worth the trouble. At Pfeiffer, the sea blasts through blowholes and caves, curls roughly around the sea stacks that were once part of its rocky cliffs, and crashes with undiminished energy on the sandy beach. It's an exhilarating, windy, bird-spangled place that epitomizes the essentially wild character of Big Sur. Ironically, this was the first place settled by white people. In 1869, the Michael Pfeiffer family built their first home here.

Pfeiffer Beach (left) and Big Sur redwoods (right), viewed from the interior of a burnt-out giant.

FLOWERS OF BIG SUR

One of Big Sur's smaller citizens gallivants across the sand, etching a tiny highway of his own.

A perennial of the sunflower family, the yellow gum plant is found on bluffs and in marshes along the coast.

One of the colorful surprises of Big Sur sand dunes and beaches is the sand-verbena, a delicate pink bloom with sticky, fat little leaves.

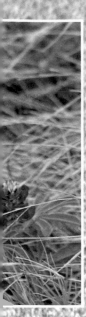

What's the secret of Big Sur flowers? Big Sur fog, which waters a rainbow of varieties up and down the coast: from orange California poppies, to the deep blue Douglas iris and purple lupine, pictured here. The silky-leaved lupine, widespread throughout the two coastal counties, is the official flower of San Luis Obispo County.

Every now and then, you'll see the fiery exclamation points of the paintbrush flower along Highway One.

To reduce erosion and maintenance on Highway One, engineers planted 86 miles of roadway with wildflowers and with ice plant, pictured. A succulent annual from South Africa, ice plant has flowers from white to brilliant pinky-red.

NEPENTHE AND THE HENRY MILLER LIBRARY

88 / 51 Just south of Pfeiffer-Big Sur State Park, the road begins to rollercoaster as it nears the coast. On Post Hill, you'll pass Post Ranch, homesteaded in the 1860s and at various times a stagecoach stop, post office and school for Big Sur. The ranch has witnessed history of a far earlier sort also. Recent excavation has turned up the first ritual grave ever found of an Esselen Indian, circa 1000 b.c.

Almost everyone stops at Nepenthe, and with good reason. This intimate point, 808 feet above sea level, overlooks an incomparable stretch of turquoise ocean. On the hill once sat a log cabin owned by Orson Welles and his wife Rita Hayworth, who divorced before ever sharing it. Later purchasers commissioned Rowan Maiden, a Frank Lloyd Wright disciple, to build a restaurant around the cabin. They named the spot "Nepenthe" after an island of the same name in a Norman Douglas novel. (Nepenthe — a Greek word meaning "sorrow banisher" — was a potion used by the ancient Greeks to give forgetfulness of pain.)

Nepenthe's famous redwood sculptures continue the classical Greek theme. The *Dark Angel* atop the gift shop was carved by Cyril Brown, longtime Big Sur resident and artist. On the upper terrace is a redwood and bronze-legged Phoenix bird, which took Edmund Kara seven months to carve.

About one-fourth mile south of Nepenthe, you'll find further evidence of the artistic creativity that Big Sur seems to stimulate. Tucked among the redwoods is a memorial library to Henry Miller, Big Sur's bohemian icon. This talented painter and writer, whose frank books (e.g. *Tropic of Cancer)* were banned in the US for decades, came to Big Sur in 1944. Here he found acceptance, kindred spirits and a niche in which to create some of his best work. Like a true artist, he also found free rent: he and friends lived for several years in the abandoned convict labor camp at Anderson Creek.

Miller left his personal library to longtime friend and fellow nonconformist Emil White. White in turn has donated it to the Big Sur Land Trust for preservation and public enjoyment. A well-known painter of mystical themes, White is also the author of the first guidebooks ever written about Big Sur. The library is free; hours vary.

Writer Henry Miller called Emil White "the only friend who never failed me." Emil came to the Big Sur country in 1943 to paint, write and ultimately to establish a library in Miller's honor. There he lives in Graves Canyon, surrounded by his naive paintings, Henry Miller's personal library, and Miller's watercolor poems, such as that in the picture, below left.

The phoenix bird — mythological symbol of rebirth — dominates the terrace of the Nepenthe restaurant. The sculpture perches on the stump of a great old oak which once shaded the property.

ANDERSON CREEK

"All the coast passed this day is very bold; there is a great swell and the land is very high. There are mountains which seem to reach the heavens, and the sea beats on them. Sailing along close to land, it appears as though they would fall on the ships."
— *from the journal of Spanish explorer Juan Cabrillo, describing the Big Sur coast as he sailed past in 1542.*

LEWIS JOSSELYN; from PAT HATHAWAY COLLECTION

It took nearly 22 years of bulldozing, blasting and grading to carve Highway One from the deeply scissored coast of Big Sur. This photo was taken in the 1930s.

79 / 60 Cabrillo was more accurate than he knew. The Santa Lucia Mountains, which give Big Sur its bold and serrated coastline, are still in motion. Part of this is man's meddling, of course. Since the highway was built, there have been dozens of major slides and countless minor ones. Pictured at right is the 1983 slide near Anderson Creek and the reconstruction of the highway.

Part of today's problem, highway officials say, relates to the amount of blasting done in the 1930s. It fractured the rock in many places and made it more volatile.

These circumstances simply make Highway One more of an adventure, a place where you can readily see the continuing struggle between the natural and the man-made.

LIMEKILN CREEK

64 / 75 One of the few industries to ever take hold along Big Sur was the gathering of tanbark oak, used in dyeing and other processes. Anderson Creek's tight little canyon was once filled with these trees. By the late 1800s, they were all harvested, as were the oaks at Notley's Landing, Bixby Canyon, Partington Canyon and other sites.

Lime smelting was another of the Big Sur coast's short-lived economic enterprises. At Bixby Creek and here at Limekiln Creek, the lime was smelted in four large kilns and brought in buckets by aerial cable to a chute, where it poured into boats waiting below. You can still see the kilns of the Rockland Cement Company by walking up a half-mile trail through the redwoods.

Engineers for the Division of Highways found this point a particular challenge. Some 163,000 cubic yards of rock had to be removed for each 1,000 feet around the point. Much of the rock was blasted laterally out to sea, using huge charges of dynamite that weighed up to 70,000 pounds.

Although pickings are pretty scarce these days, rockhounds enjoy looking in Limekiln Creek and along the small beach for jade, jaspar, agates and garnets.

During their brief heyday, four kilns roared with flame, producing smelted lime. Originally brought in by ship, the kilns now stand in a picturesque jungle of vines and creepers. The interior is shot from the ground looking up the chimney.

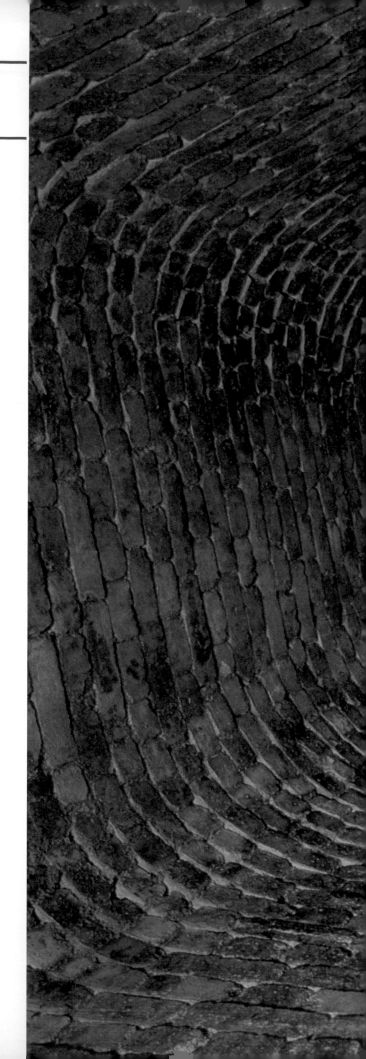

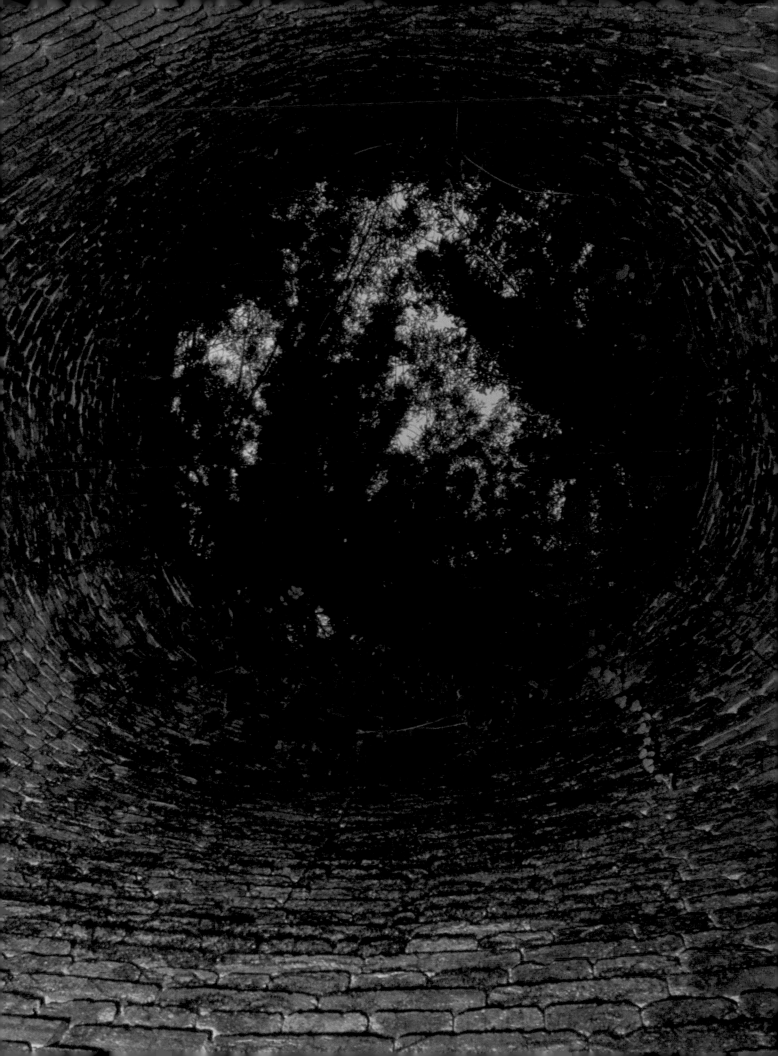

KIRK CREEK and MILL CREEK

61 / 78 Fifty years ago, a road camp to house convict labor occupied the gentle green point at Kirk Creek. Today you can camp on the same sunny bluff where the little houses once stood. Instead of cabins, you'll find flowers in abundance, including California's own golden poppy.

During the building of Highway One, three labor camps came into being. The first was near Little Sur River; the second, at Kirk Creek. Two crews (composed of convicts and free men) worked towards one another. When north and south crews met at Big Creek about 1934, the camps at Little Sur and Kirk Creek were consolidated into one at Anderson Creek.

These camps housed about 150 of San Quentin's "best be-haved" inmates. For their manual labor, the workers were paid in money (from 35 to 75 cents per day) and/or in "good time." Good time shortened their sentences three days for each two days' work on the road.

At Little Sur, prison officials put the former captain of Califor-nia's 1902 football team in charge. Basically, however, the camps were run on the honor system — no uniforms, no gun-carrying

PAT HATHAWAY COLLECTION

guards. Escape attempts were few, no doubt due to the discouraging terrain.

The prisoners were allowed a certain amount of self-expression in their living quarters. Many took pride in customizing their little shacks. Some grew vegetable gardens or roses. Other enterprising souls built a moonshine still or two!

Between Kirk and Mill Creek, you will cross the Nacimiento-Ferguson Road, the only route east to Mission San Antonio and to US Highway 101. It is mountainous, scenic and open sporadically, so inquire before setting out. At Mill Creek, the jade bulk of the Santa Lucia Mountains looms behind the boulder-strewn beach. About 15 million years ago, the Santa Lucias were not mountains at all but one of three islands in an inland sea covering central California. Then the Pacific tectonic plate pushed under the North American plate, causing a fiery upheaval that brought the Santa Lucias into being.

The Mill Creek Bridge (right) has had its difficulties. Stormy weather in 1956 caused this bizarre "flaps down" collapse.

SAND DOLLAR BEACH AND JADE COVE

57
82

The austere, dun-colored south coast supports two pint-sized communities: Pacific Valley, once a center for Los Burros Mining District, and Gorda. The latter got its fetching Spanish name of "gorda" or "fat woman" from a large offshore rock. If you squint just so, it does have a vague resemblance to a plump female body.

Between Pacific Valley and Gorda are two rewarding stops. The first is Sand Dollar Beach, a lovely white crescent noted for the hang-gliding from its bluffs. You can camp within walking distance at Plaskett Creek Campground.

About one mile south begin a series of coves, invisible from the road and marked only by dirt pulloffs and a small brown sign. Collectively called Jade Cove, this stretch of coast between Plaskett Point and Willow Creek is reached by a stairway down 150-foot cliffs. (Slightly easier access is via Willow Creek Beach, at the south end.)

In centuries past, Chinese junks collected green and golden jade along here. More than $1 million worth of the soapy-feeling stone has been taken from this area. In 1971, three divers worked for months to retrieve what turned out to be a superlative for the *Guinness Book of World Records:* a boulder of nephrite jade that weighed 9,000 pounds, measured 8½ by 5 feet, and was valued at $180,000.

Your finds will probably be more modest. Best pickings occur at low tides and after storms. Jade Cove is also littered with much less valuable green and black serpentine.

Alive, the sand dollar is covered with an unremarkable grey-green fur. Dead, it dries to become a beautiful star-shaped skeleton. Sand dollars are both first cousins and a food source to starfish.

SPRUCE CREEK TO CARPOFORO CREEK

40 / 99 High above the ocean, you encounter the slowest, most savage terrain of Highway One. (Fortunately, you will also encounter several waterfall-supplied drinking fountains at 4 to 6-mile intervals. These small pulloffs are a welcome breather along this arid stretch.)

Between Spruce Creek and the Monterey-San Luis Obispo County line, be prepared to move at what the highway department calls "a scenic crawl" — an average speed of 30 mph.

As you negotiate the endless curves, your co-pilot might amuse you with the following tidbits. In the 65 miles of heaviest construction which you are traversing, over 10 million cubic yards of rock were blasted away. At any given time, five huge shovels worked the highway, each moving 1,500 cubic yards a day. At least one power shovel ended up in the ocean. Villa Creek Bridge, one of the otherwise unremarkable bridges you cross, was the target of wartime sabotage. In 1945, highway workers found 38 sticks of dynamite hidden under it.

Whether you are headed north or south, winsome Ragged Point makes an appropriate stop. Its greenness is a relief to the eye, just as its food, lodging and bathroom facilities are a relief to other portions of your anatomy. Aromatic with eucalyptus and peppery nasturiums, Ragged Point's park makes a fine place to watch the fog burn off in that peculiar and balmy Big Sur fashion.

A mile south of Ragged Point is Carpoforo Creek, tucked against the green ankles of the Santa Lucia Mountains. In physical appearances anyway, this is the "official" beginning of the Big Sur coastal landscape.

In 1769, four scouts with the Portolá expedition accidentally got separated from their group near Carmel. They wandered south for 18 days, ending up more dead than alive near this beautiful creek. Kindly Salinan Indians dusted them off, fed them and pointed them in the right direction to rejoin their party. The scouts' mistake marked the first crossing of the Big Sur country by white men.

The many moods of the sea: blowholes, waves and wind-stirred open water. From above, the water off Big Sur produces colors to match its moods — from the milky turquoise of the shallows to the cold blue-grey deep.

PIEDRAS BLANCAS

33 **106** Piedras Blancas was built on its headland in 1874 and stands sentinel 145 feet above the ocean. Prior to that, the point merely had a rustic lookout tower for whales and ships in distress. Three white fangs emerge from the rough waters at its base, guano-white islets that give Piedras Blancas — "white rocks" in Spanish — its name.

Captain Thorndyke, the first lighthouse keeper, maintained the 5-wick, kerosene vapor lamp for 30 years. In 1906 he quit, saying he couldn't stand the noise of the newfangled foghorn. Now automated, Piedras Blancas once used a superb Fresnel lens visible for 18 miles. You can see the lens at close hand in Cambria, near the little jail in the west section of the village.

Since the mid-1970s, Piedras Blancas has served as a base for marine wildlife studies. Federal researchers have studied the sea otter and the kelp forests in which they spend most of their lives.

South of the lighthouse is a small bay where you can see quantities of kelp, which colors the sea like a great bruise. This member of the brown algae family grows to 100 feet, anchoring itself to the ocean floor and using air bladders to bring its leaves to the surface. The kelp forest is sanctuary for numerous fish and various marine creatures, including the sea otter. Kelp is also the favorite snack of the prickly sea urchins that populate the sea floor.

Piedras Blancas (also pictured on the cover) is a prime spot to watch sea otters.

SAN SIMEON AND HEARST CASTLE

27
112

In 1769, Gaspar de Portolá and his expedition of Spanish soldiers camped at San Simeon point, noting its fine possibilities as a port. One hundred years later, miner-turned-millionaire George Hearst began buying land here, ending up with a cattle ranch bigger than some European countries.

It was San Simeon's pier and good harbor that made possible the building of Hearst Castle, begun in 1919 by George's son, William Randolph. As his architect, he chose Julia Morgan. She soon concluded that all materials would need to be brought in by boat.

It cost nearly $3 million in 1930s dollars to build the 4-floor, 100-room Casa Grande. Everything was hauled up six miles of bad road, heavy items taking half a day each.

It's estimated that this living museum, built to house WRH's art treasures from around the world, cost about $10 million. Looked at another way, it cost as much to build and furnish Hearst Castle as it did to build this 139- mile stretch of Highway One.

Because the highway was to pass through Hearst property, builders needed a right-of-way from WRH. Initially reluctant, Hearst was won over by the persuasiveness and persistence of State Senator Rigdon and Monterey Supervisor Dr. John Roberts, the moving forces behind the highway.

San Simeon was a busy shipping point for the activities of the south coast: mining, whaling, dairying, seaweed-gathering. In a typical year (1878), San Simeon pier shipped:

3,934 boxes of butter

930 firkins and barrels of butter

26,385 pounds of wool

250 boxes of eggs

169 flasks of quicksilver

94 coops of fowl

5,350 calf hides

374 beef hides

299 packages of whale oil

725 tons of grain

14 barrels of tallow

104 neats of seaweed

169 sacks of abalone

1,277 miscellaneous packages

HEARST CASTLE

27 / 112 The pools and grounds of Hearst Castle offer as much to impress and astonish as the buildings themselves.

Pictured here is the 345,000-gallon Neptune Pool, dominated by its ancient Greco-Roman temple façade.

Its indoor companion, the Roman pool, took five years and nearly $400,000 to build. The main pool alone absorbed half a million hand-set tiles in real gold leaf and lapis lazuli.

To landscape the castle, a 20-man crew hauled a mountain of topsoil to form five terrace levels atop the hill. Among other things, they planted 3,000 rose-bushes and over 100,000 trees, including the mature 30-foot cypresses you see around the Neptune Pool area.

The winding approach to the castle has its own surprises. During Hearst's day, he assembled the largest private zoo in the world. Over 70 species roamed on 2,000 fenced-in acres. More exotic breeds had special enclosures. Although the ostriches, giraffes and tigers are gone, you can still glimpse an occasional zebra or tahr goat on these tranquil slopes.

HEARST CASTLE

27 / 112 A favorite with visitors and with its creator, the Refectory (originally called "the Dining Room") glows with medieval welcome. One end of the 67-foot room is anchored by a 27-foot-high French Gothic fireplace, whose mouth is spacious enough to walk into, should anyone ever have wanted to carry out that odd notion.

The walls are paneled with 15th century Spanish choir stalls and 16th century Flemish tapestries of wool and silk. Hearst amassed a brilliant collection of tapestries — nearly 4,000 square feet of them hang in the Castle. A newspaper publisher himself, perhaps he was drawn by their story-telling qualities.

Although medieval in mood, the Refectory is far from gloomy. The room sparkles with some of WRH's choicest treasures — notably his fine silver, worth an incalculable amount even in his day. More gaiety is added by the 24 Palio banners, which bear the crests of the noble families of Siena, Italy. The Refectory's final touch of color can be spotted on the monastery tables. At intervals, bottles of catsup and mustard sit, a homely reminder of the simple beginnings of life at "the ranch," as Hearst always called it.

CAMBRIA

19 120 North and south of Cambria, the coast is horizontal, a series of gentle marine terraces backed by tawny grazing land. At Cambria, the terrain changes abruptly. The land splits into valleys, upholstered with velvety hills small and large. Both hills and dales are furred with Monterey pines (*Pinus radiata*), a fog-loving, wind-twisted variety native to just four small places in the world.

The village temperament is as distinctive as its setting. Cambria has a decided British air, from its pubs and Tudor timbering to its street names and its teams of white-suited lawn bowlers. Thanks to the large number of artists and retirees who live here, Cambria offers an unvillagelike array of cultural activities.

Driftwood collecting is especially fine and easy to do at San Simeon and Moonstone Beaches on Cambria's north shoulder.

MORRO BAY

0 / 139

Twenty million years ago, give or take an eon, volcanic activity created Morro Rock and the beautiful vertebrae of eight peaks that wind their way through San Luis Obispo County.

Long a landmark for explorers, Morro Rock stands 576 feet high, a stocky sentry at the mouth of a pyramid-shaped bay. A five-mile finger of white sand points at the rock, almost landlocking Morro Bay's mouth.

On the sandspit, you'll marvel at dunes 85 feet high, the wealth of bird life, and 100 plant species. The southeast side also harbors great shell mounds or middens, left by the Chumash Indians 200 to 500 years ago. It's clear to see that the Chumash dined well. Their ancient garbage includes bent-nosed clams, gaper clams, basket cockles, littlenecks, moon snails and native oysters. (The oysters died out in the 1930s, due to increased salinity in the Bay. Today we must be content with *Crasotrea gigas,* the rather ordinary cultivated oyster.)

An important albacore port, Morro Bay also fishes in an easy-going way for tourists. It's an open secret that locals enjoy the rock, the wharf, and the bay every bit as much as their visitors.

Five hundred years after the picnic: Chumash Indian shell mounds or middens reveal abalone, oyster shells, cockles, clams and other edible species.

MORRO BAY

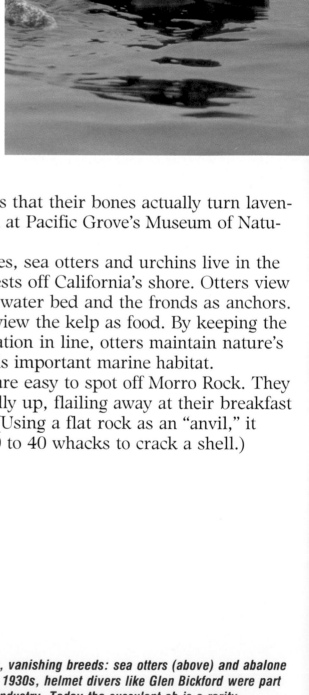

0
139

The size and relatively unpolluted state of Morro Bay make it a prime wildlife sanctuary. Among its residents are sea otters. These droll, mustachioed mammals have devised a novel adaptation to the sea. Unlike seals, they have no blubber for buoyancy or protection against the cold. To keep afloat, they constantly roll in the water, which pushes air into their fur. To keep warm, they eat. And eat. And eat. Every day, a 40- to 60-pound adult otter puts away 25% of his body weight in groceries.

Sea otters have received a lot of bad press about their teenagerlike appetites. The truth is, otters dine on a wide menu — and on many items rarely consumed by Americans. Sea urchins may be the otters' favorite. They eat so many of the purple urchins that their bones actually turn lavender with age! (Scoffers should study the otter skeleton at Pacific Grove's Museum of Natural History.)

Along with hundreds of fish and other marine species, sea otters and urchins live in the vast kelp forests off California's shore. Otters view the kelp as a water bed and the fronds as anchors. The urchins view the kelp as food. By keeping the urchin population in line, otters maintain nature's balance in this important marine habitat.

Sea otters are easy to spot off Morro Rock. They often float belly up, flailing away at their breakfast with a rock. (Using a flat rock as an "anvil," it takes them 10 to 40 whacks to crack a shell.)

Threatened species, vanishing breeds: sea otters (above) and abalone divers (left). In the 1930s, helmet divers like Glen Bickford were part of a thriving local industry. Today the succulent ab is a rarity. California sea otters, hunted to virtual extinction for their glossy pelts, now number about 1,300. Despite legal protection, their survival is also precarious.

MORRO BAY ESTUARY

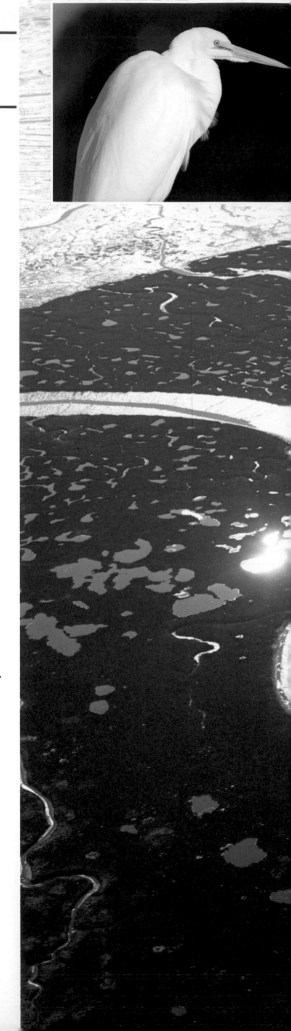

0 / 139

The arithmetic of the Morro Bay estuary:
- 1,452 acres of mudflats
- 22 miles of channels at low tide
- water temperatures from 50° to 64° F
- 250 species of birds
- 18 species of clams and bivalves
- 66 species of fish

But none of these figures can begin to draw a picture of this silver-veined meeting place of fresh and salt water. A recycling organism, a nursery, a refuge, a major source of food — the estuary is all of these. Half the sea creatures harvested on the Pacific Coast depend on estuaries. They come here to give birth, to grow up, to rest, to hide, to eat.

The Morro Bay estuary is a critical rest stop for tired birds along the Great Pacific Flyway. As many as 11,800 black brants have been counted at a time, usually with heads bent to nibble eel grass, their favorite fast food. Any time of year, the estuary is dotted with snowy egrets, lost in thought. Ruddy turnstones looking for crab. Great blue herons hanging against long-fingered eucalyptus trees. Buffleheads and widgeons and curlews and cormorants.

Twice a day, the estuary fills with what looks like water. Smell it, and you'll discover it is a rich soup of microscopic life, a reek of burning iodine and halibut spawn and millions of particles of decomposing eel grass.

More than anything, the estuary is a theatre of nature whose performances are often invisible to our coarse vision. If you could peer to the bottom, you'd see:
- oysters gravely pumping the estuary broth through their filters at a steady 8 gallons per hour;
- the fat innkeeper, a rotund pink worm who hospitably opens his large burrow to transients like the pea crab, the scaleworm and the goby fish;
- the geoduck, a paranoid clam with a great leathery neck a foot long, who carefully extends his nose and makes a burrow for his relatively insignificant body deep in the black mud.

Morro Bay estuary is dotted with egrets, who stand poised, lost in thought.

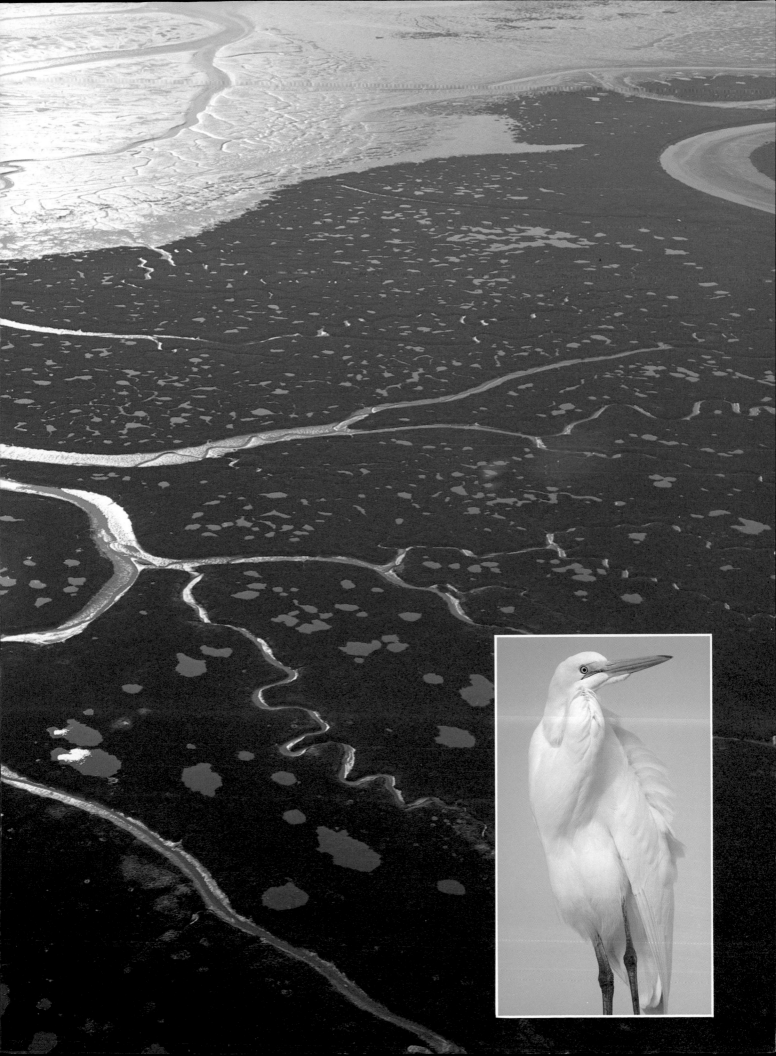

The invisible theater of the estuary.
The sharp emerald triangles of the Big Sur coast.
The wave-swept rocks and cypresses
of the Monterey peninsula.

All of them contain a rich concentrate of nature's glory. Human beings seem to need this beauty as much as they need food and sleep. But nature's gifts have a string attached — a string called responsibility.

In the tidepools of California lives a small, restless creature called the hermit crab. A homely fellow without a shell of his own, he borrows the cast-off finery of others. From time to time, he grows bored or too big for his glossy moon shell or periwinkle and leaves it for another hermit crab to discover.

To preserve this fair coast and the slender ribbon of Highway One that edges it, we need to take a page from the hermit crab's book. We must insinuate ourselves into this environment as gently as the hermit crab. We can borrow its beauty for awhile and then pass on, leaving behind an unsullied marvel for the restless creatures of future human generations to enjoy.